MAP KENWYN:

THE LIFE AND TIMES
OF CECIL BEER

by

GARRY TREGIDGA AND TREVE CRAGO

FIRST PUBLISHED IN 2000
BY GORSETH KERNOW

ISBN 1-903668-00-X

British Library Cataloguing in Publication Data
A catalogue record for this book
is available from the British Library

Designed by Ray Lancefield
The Design Field, Truro, Cornwall
ray@thedesignfield.com

Printed by R. Booth (Bookbinders) Ltd
Mabe Burnthouse, Penryn, Cornwall

FOREWORD

I would like to commend this publication to you as the first in a series on individuals who have been bards of Gorseth Kernow, and have contributed in various ways to the distinct identity, history, language and culture of Cornwall.

Major Cecil Herbert Beer, Map Kenwyn, was made a bard in 1934, only six years after the creation of Gorseth Kernow in 1928. He died in 1998, after a long life of service to Cornwall, through the seminal group, Tyr ha Tavas, and as an early member of Mebyon Kernow, where he was for a short time its chairman. He was on the Gorseth Council where he served for many years. He attended council meetings and contributed with spirit and common sense until just before his death. He was Deputy Grand Bard from 1967-1972. I remember him as a kindly, generous-minded man, who fought fiercely for the Cornwall he loved, and supported all those who felt as he did. He was particularly kind to me in the 1950's when I was struggling to learn Cornish! His life is in a sense, a mirror of the development of Gorseth Kernow and other bodies through the twentieth century.

In his later years, he emigrated to Australia to be near some of his family, only returning again in the nineties. When in Australia, he was active in the formation and running of the first gorseth assembly there, and in several others which followed at two yearly intervals at the Kernewek Lowender.

Map Kenwyn was a man of wide ranging talents, political activist, Cornish language speaker, Gorseth bard and deputy leader. This publication is in part his memorial.

I am very grateful to Dr Garry Tregidga for producing this brief biography, amidst the many concerns and commitments he has as deputy director of the Institute of Cornish Studies, also to Treve Crago who is working on Gorseth archival research as well as Senior Researcher for the Cornish Audio Visual Archive project, and to the Gorseth itself for producing this publication.

Bryallen, Barth Mur
Ann Trevenen Jenkin, Grand Bard
Leedstown, June 2000.

Map Kenwyn 1902-1998

MAP KENWYN:
THE LIFE AND TIMES OF CECIL BEER

INTRODUCTION

The death of Major Cecil Beer in April 1998 marked the loss of one of our few living links with the Cornish movement of the inter-war period. These years form a vital period in the evolution of the Celtic Revival, as a younger generation moved away from the antiquarian interests of earlier pioneers to a more populist movement which could reach out to the general public. Beer symbolised this transition. Indeed, as secretary of Tyr ha Tavas (Land and Language), a group of young language and cultural enthusiasts in the 1930s, he played a significant role in developments. This study will concentrate on Beer's vital background role in that organisation, partly because it was the main focus of a recorded interview with him at the end of 1996 and also because it is a rather neglected aspect of the Revivalist era. Beer, however, continued to play a part in the development of the Cornish movement after the Second World War, serving as chairman of Mebyon Kernow (1956-60) and deputy Grand Bard of the Gorseth Kernow (1967-72). This study will therefore consider his achievements against the background of wider developments relating to Cornish culture and ethno regionalism throughout the twentieth century.

FROM CECIL BEER TO MAP KENWYN: A QUEST FOR IDENTITY

Cecil Herbert Beer was born at Putney in London on 2nd October 1902. His family roots, however, were very much in Cornwall. Cecil's parents, Harry Herbert and Elisa Beer, originally had a drapery business in Truro and he was related to the Tippetts and Blewetts, the well-known local bakers. He was brought up in a rather comfortable middle-class family, receiving an elementary and secondary education before studying at St George's College in London. He then took an examination to join the Civil Service, in which he obtained the highest marks in Britain in that particular year, and during the inter-war years he worked for the War Office and then the Post Office Savings Bank. His personal interests were varied. In his youth he was one of the early members of the Scout Movement, while he took a great interest in athletics and field archaeology. Beer also had a deep religious faith. He was raised in a Christian household, and in August 1927 he married Winifred Robinson, a member of his local Baptist Church in Wimbledon, after meeting her at church choir practice.[1]

The other love of his life was undoubtedly Cornwall. An opportunity to take a greater interest in Cornish affairs came with the formation of Tyr ha Tavas in 1932. This, as Beer wrote, was the 'brainchild' of Edmund Hambly of Port Isaac just before he left the Duchy to become a medical student at St Bartholomew's Hospital in London. 'It is understood to have had its inception at an informal meeting of young Cornish enthusiasts which took place in the romantic setting of the cliffs of North Cornwall'.[2]

Cecil Beer (on right) in Scout uniform, 1925.

These individuals had recently left Blundell's private school in Tiverton where they had been inspired to revive Kernewek by A.S.D. Smith, the Celtic Scholar, who was their Modern Languages master at the school. As Beer put it, 'being about to leave their homeland for the Great Metropolis where their careers were planned to start, they resolved to band together and form a group dedicated to their love of Cornwall and all its heritage and in particular to foster and use Cornish as a spoken language'.[3]

Once in London, Hambly and two other medical students, his brother Trevan and M.W. Harvey, contacted E.G. Retallack Hooper, then a horticultural student at Kew, and the group became an active society with informal meetings for the exchange of ideas and discussion using the Cornish language as far as possible.

Beer was increasingly drawn into this circle of young 'Revivalists'. He was the principal organiser of the first church service in revived Cornish and after the resignation of Trelawney Roberts, the secretary of Tyr ha Tavas, Beer became an integral member of An Tredden, the group's inner circle of three leaders, as General Secretary and Treasurer. Many of the ideas initiated by Tyr ha Tavas were apparently developed by Beer, such as Christmas cards written in Cornish, a trade mark for Cornish products and the group's Chough logo.[4] Beer also reflected the changing nature of the movement in regard to religion. Many of the older revivalists like Henry Jenner and Canon Doble were either Roman Catholics or High Anglicans, and their romantic objective, as Payton explained, was to 'rebuild a pre-industrial Celtic-Catholic culture in Cornwall'.[5] This created the potential for a cultural clash with the Methodist majority in the Duchy. Yet Tyr ha Tavas was a symbol of the broader movement which now existed. It included high Anglicans, but the principal organisers like Beer and Hambly were nonconformists. Hambly, a Quaker, declared in 1933 that it was a tragedy that John Wesley had not lived a century earlier since the 'religious zeal that he aroused might have arrested the decay of the language' if it had been used in religious services. He added that 'one can easily picture the eloquence the local preachers might have reached in the use of the native tongue'.[6]

This attempt to popularise the Revival was evident with Beer's work in organising church services and concerts conducted in the Cornish language. A key aim of Tyr ha Tavas was to encourage the use of Cornish in the wider community and by acting as a ginger group in collaboration with other organisations, such as the Gorseth and the Federation of Old Cornwall Societies, Tyr ha Tavas was able to achieve some successes. The group developed the idea of an annual church service in Cornish during the 1930s, the first of which in revived Cornish was held at Towednack church in 1933. As was so typical of his unassuming personality throughout his long life Beer preferred not to be in the limelight at this event, but was content to remain in the background quietly but resolutely ensuring its smooth running. Without doubt the service was a significant success and can be seen as something of a landmark in respect of drawing the general public's attention to the existence of a blossoming Cornish language movement. The novelty of the event attracted a considerable amount of coverage from the local press, with the *Western Morning News* reporting that 'strange as were the words to the majority of the congregation the service went with remarkable facility and before the close the congregation joined in the singing of the hymns'.[7]

Within Towednack's small oil-lit church the congregation was swelled by the ranks of the Tyr ha Tavas members who were holding their first camp in Cornwall at Trevail Farm near Zennor. The choir for the service actually consisted of some dozen young people from the organisation. Also present were the Breton wrestling team who the previous day had taken part in a match against the Cornish wrestlers at the Redruth Rugby Ground under the supervision of Tregoning Hooper (Bras Y Golon), Secretary of the Cornwall County Wrestling Association, and Dr Cotonnec, President of the Comite des Luttes et des Sports Athletiques de la Cornouaille. Reports of the service remarked how the Bretons clearly understood all the readings and sermons being delivered by Tyr ha Tavas members Trevan Hambly, E.E Morton Nance and A.S.D Smith. Later the young Breton wrestlers were to spend some time at the Tyr Ha Tavas camp conversing with the enthusiastic Cornish speakers.[8]

The service was conducted by the Rev Leslie Verne Jolly who was himself barded in 1935 at Penzance taking the bardic name of Pronter Jolyf (Ready Priest). Subsequently, Tyr ha Tavas camps and church services held in the Cornish language became a regular fixture in the revivalist calendar during the years leading up to the Second World War.

Logo of Tyr Ha Tavas.

Tyr ha Tavas under Beer's steady influence strived not only to avoid becoming an elitist organisation but also made a concerted effort to make its activities affordable for all. This was illustrated by the costing of the 1935 camp which was held at St Cleer, with Beer remarking in the organisation's annual report that the 'all in' expenses for that particular year's camp had only amounted to 17s 11d per person for the week.[9]

In this particular year newspaper reports reveal that it was Cecil Beer and Edmund Hambly together who led the Tyr ha Tavas members in procession to the Cornish service in Liskeard Parish Church from their camp on the downs[10] The *Cornish Guardian* acknowledged that the general organisation was in the 'capable hands' of Mr Beer.[11] Perhaps an explanation for Beer's enthusiasm and expertise in arranging such events is that he was a pioneer member of the Scout movement having reputedly attended one of Baden Powell's first Boy Scout camps held on Brownsea Island. The popularity of the church service itself grew so much during the inter-war years that when it was held at Launceston in 1938 over 400 members of the public attended. Similarly, the programme for a concert at Bodmin broadcast by the BBC in 1936 was printed in both English and Cornish. A broadcast concert in the previous year actually had a number of items by St Austell Male Voice Choir performed in the Cornish language. Francis Tredinnick in a letter to Beer in June 1935 claimed that this populist approach was the way to preserve the nation's distinctive heritage:

'I was so thrilled at the **Cornish** broadcast last Tuesday that I felt compelled to write to the Choir in appreciation. This morning I received a letter and Press Reports from Hoey. He says he has been successful in getting seven choirs in Cornwall to sing in Cornish. Once we get the Cornish singing in Cornish (whether they understand the words or not), we shall have achieved our object. That little extra symbolism will prevent us (in spite of the Movies and the Talkies) from going down to posterity as variants of the ZummerZetZhire village idiots.'[12]

Beer himself was able to persuade a local newspaper to print bilingual short stories, while he got the Three Burrows Music Festival to hold a class in the Cornish language. These are clear examples of the progress that the Cornish language was making during the 1930s and the long term influence of this renaissance of interest in Cornish identity has proven to be influential on contemporary officers of the Gorseth.

John Jenkin, the current secretary of the Cornish Gorseth, remembers attending the Three Burrows festival encouraged by his enthusiastic uncle, Edwin Chirgwin (Map Melyn):

> 'Uncle Edwin didn't have any children and he was very keen to get his nephews interested and the three of us in fact, we three spoke our first Cornish at the age of about nine at the Three Burrows Music and Elocution Festival...didn't understand it but we stood up at this festival and recited a poem or something in Cornish.'[13]

It appears that Beer was also instrumental in keeping Tyr ha Tavas in existence during the decade. As an organisation it was faced with many problems during its comparatively short existence. Its maximum membership was apparently less than one hundred, although there were others who sympathised with its aims. About two-thirds of activists, including leaders like Hambly and Beer, lived outside Cornwall. The group found it difficult to establish branches in the Duchy, while three of its principal branches outside the area, at Kent, Bristol and Bournemouth, were effectively independent. This problem was made worse by a lack of funds. Many members did not even pay the annual subscription of a shilling, and Beer had to subsidise the group's activities from his own income, particularly the circular sent to members. It was no coincidence that Tyr ha Tavas effectively collapsed when Beer, who was on the officers reserve list, was called up for military service on the immediate outbreak of war in September 1939.[14]

Cecil Beer throughout this period had been diligently mastering the Cornish language. On a dull and misty day high upon Padderbury Top near Liskeard on Friday September 7th 1934 he was initiated as a Bard of the Cornish Gorseth, taking the bardic name of Map Kenwyn, (Son of Kenwyn). He had successfully gained his right to this honour through examination in the Cornish language, which during this era meant producing a 500 word essay in Kernewek of suitable quality and was barded alongside fellow Tyr ha Tavas members Francis Cargeeg (Deputy Grand Bard 1962-67) and Ernest Morton Nance (Deputy Grand Bard 1982-88). The Padderbury Top Gorseth is notable for another significant event because it was at this ceremony that Robert Morton Nance (Mordon) was installed as Grand Bard following the death of Henry Jenner on May 1st earlier that year. This event, as *The Cornish Times* observed, generated considerable local excitement:

> 'Long before the Gorsedd opened Liskeard, the nearest centre, was crowded with motor vehicles, and the narrow winding lanes leading through Pengover and
> Doddy Cross to Padderbury were thick with traffic. The Bards, numbering nearly 60 men and women, came from all over Cornwall and even as far afield as London and Yorkshire. They first assembled at Liskeard Public hall, and having donned their flowing sky blue robes and hoods motored to the Gorsedd site. There with the 13 initiates leading the way, they walked in procession up the gentle slope to the summit of the hill where their arrival was awaited with interest by many hundreds of members of Old Cornwall Societies who had travelled from all parts of the county.'[15]

Mordon was then installed as Grand Bard 'with simple dignity' by the Deputy Grand Bard J Hambly Rowe (Tolzethan). It is also notable that this, the seventh Cornish Gorseth, was the first held without the assistance of Bards from other Celtic nations. From the evidence of the ceremony's success it can be argued that this absence not only reveals the extent of the significant growth of participation in the Cornish revivalist movement in terms of actual physical numbers during this era, but is also an indicator of an increasing self confidence that the Cornish were developing in their own specific Celtic identity. This point was recognised by Canon H.R Jennings (Saws Degemerys) who was the official Gorseth speaker:

'Not yet of course has the Cornish Gorsedd captured the heart of Cornwall as it has in Wales where they carry on their ceremonies for a whole week and are greeted by tens of thousands of enthusiastic spectators. They have 150 years of renewed life behind them; we are only six years old. But year by year the roll of the Cornish Bards grows longer and gradually we are covering the whole life of the county as one by one the leaders honour the bardic circle by accepting the invitation to receive the honour of a bard. And each year young people qualify for admission by passing the examination in the Cornish language.'[16]

Souvenir programme of Padderbury.

UNCERTAIN ASPIRATIONS: POLITICS AND THE REVIVALIST MOVEMENT

Yet members of the inter-war Cornish movement were unsure of how far they should travel in a nationalist direction. Early pioneers like Henry Jenner and the Rev. W.S. Lach-Szyrma had focused on anti-quarian efforts to reconstruct the Cornish language and on the 'study and discussion of Celtic relics'.[17] Although some individuals associated with the Liberal party were already using the cultural themes raised by the Cornish movement for electoral purposes before the First World War, the Revivalists themselves tended to be strongly in favour of the political union of the British Isles. Developments after 1918 merely confirmed the antiquarian nature of the Revival. The creation of the Federation of Old Cornwall Societies in 1924 represented a serious attempt to disseminate the ideas of the movement to a wider audience, with the emphasis being placed on linking the popular interest in dialect sketches and local history to the preservation of the Celtic identity of Cornwall. But by 1935 Robert Morton Nance was expressing his concern to Beer that some local societies were even neglecting their cultural role. He added that the movement was attracting 'people who will never learn, or do, or collect, anything, but at the same time join a society because it is a Cornish one and they have a vague Cornish sentiment'.[18]

Tyr ha Tavas represented an important stage in the evolution of Cornish nationalism. Although ostensibly a language pressure group, its members placed a greater emphasis on concepts like nationality. For example, Edwin Chirgwin noted in his diary in February 1933 that Tyr ha Tavas was 'nationalist in essence'.[19] The Revivalists may still have thought primarily in terms of cultural nationalism, but wider developments and the evolution of ideas meant that there was now a natural progression to political nationalism. This was borne out by the group's constitution which stated that Tyr ha Tavas was 'an organization to unite those persons of Cornish birth or descent who value their Cornish heritage and who desire to maintain the outlook, individualism, culture and idealism that characterises their race so as to pass on the unbroken tradition. The primary aim is service to Cornwall and Cornish people and in particular it seeks: -

a. To preserve in the youth of Cornwall a love and

understanding of their country and its history.

b. To encourage an expression in drama, music art, literature and cultural forms, of the innate Cornish instinct.

c. To encourage the practice of typical Cornish sports.

d. To utilise the Cornish language both as an outward and visible sign of nationality, and as a means of helping Cornish people to realise their essential kinship with other Celtic nations. To show Cornish people what Cornishmen have done and what they can still do to help the world.'[20]

Hambly, who was apparently related by marriage to the Rowntree family, used his social contacts to put pressure on the Cornish MPs to tackle social and economic problems in the Duchy. He encouraged members of the group to take an active interest in the 'social conditions and industry of the motherland. It was their desire to see that the education, the daily and industrial life... was the best that Cornwall could provide'.[21] By the end of the decade activists were starting to link their defence of the culture of 'our ancient kingdom', as they put it, to the national struggles of other ethnic minorities:

'Does the Jew wish to keep his Passover? Make his existence a burden to him!
Does the Basque wish to maintain his national characteristics? Decimate him!
Does the Breton wish to preserve his language? Ban it from public instruction! Is there a Cornishman who is interested in the ancient tongue of Cornwall? Tell him that he is wasting his time...! There is a tendency everywhere ...to crush personal and national individuality.'[22]

Some younger members of Tyr ha Tavas, such as Francis Cargeeg and Retallack Hooper, wanted the organisation to have clear political objectives from the very beginning, thereby copying Plaid Cymru which linked the defence of the Welsh language to the political goal of self-government.[23] Both men were associated with the Labour movement. Cargeeg was an active trade unionist at Plymouth dockyard at this time, and was increasingly concerned with the social problems of Cornwall. However, such individuals appeared to have been something of a rarity in the Duchy as Richard Jenkin remembers in relation to Cargeeg's links with John Legonna:

> 'John Legonna who was older than the normal under-graduate, he would probably be about 28 in 1943. And he refused to serve in the army as a Cornish and Welsh nationalist... and somehow he got deferred and went to Oxford and studied under A.L Rowse. A.L Rowse mentions him somewhere in one of his books, not by name but by one of his students who used to go round Cornwall looking for patriots...and the only one he could find was Francis Cargeeg in Hayle!'[24]

Retallack Hooper, Grand Bard of the Gorseth (1959-64) and more commonly known by his bardic name Talek, eventually became president of Mebyon Kernow (Sons of Cornwall) and played a prominent role in that organisation's early electioneering in the 1960s. A Labour supporter in the 1930s, he was an enthusiastic supporter of A.L. Rowse's attempt to develop an anti-metropolitan image for the social-ist party. In an article in *Cornish Labour News* Talek put forward the idea of a new 'Cornish Socialism' that combined a locally-based approach to socio-economic problems with active support for the nation's Celtic heritage. Appropriately enough, he concluded with the slogan 'Omseveagh why gonesugy Kernow!' (Arise – workers of Cornwall!).[25] Rowse himself took an interest in the development of the Cornish youth group. In 1937, when he was parliamentary candi-date for Penryn & Falmouth, he declared that if Tyr ha Tavas was serious in its talk about 'Cornwall for the Cornish [and] the particular character of the Cornish people', they should give him their support because he represented their only chance of there being a Cornish Prime Minister.[26]

Beer, however, was reluctant to embrace a political agenda. Living in the prosperous county of Surrey he lacked first hand experience of the appalling social and economic problems of the Duchy.

Furthermore, he felt that the approach of Cargeeg and Talek could cause internal friction since Tyr ha Tavas had been formed with the intention of making the Cornish language and culture more accessible to the general public. It was felt that an active involvement in politics would prevent members from concentrating on its primary task. Timing was also important. The 1930s, of course, witnessed the rise of Hitler, and this meant that nationalism became, as Beer put it, a 'dirty word'.27 The Cornish MPs, now predominately Conservative, adopted a cautious attitude towards the group, while even some sympathisers were concerned that Tyr ha Tavas might move in a fascist direction. Beer, in particular, wanted the youth group to avoid a 'wildcat' image. In his view Tyr ha Tavas had to remain non-political, and in order to develop a respectable image he persuaded J.W Hunkin, the bishop of Truro, and Sir John Langdon Bonython, a wealthy Cornish exile in South Australia, to become patrons of Tyr ha Tavas. It was this respectable and essentially non-political role which was eventually accepted.

Friction within the group and with other revivalists in the wider Cornish movement also threatened the existence of Tyr ha Tavas. For example, the early resignation of Trelawney Roberts as secretary was due to a disagreement with Hambly over the direction of the movement. An even more serious crisis arose in 1935 when Hambly added the words the 'World Cornish Movement' to the group's title. His unilateral decision naturally angered other individuals, particularly Robert Morton Nance. Letters written at the time clearly show that the elders in the movement were becoming seriously concerned by the activities of the youth branch, and there was talk of an impending crisis. As Nance remarked, it was totally unacceptable that the 'centre of any Cornish movement on a world scale should be shifted into [London] which from a national point of view is a foreign capital'. Nance added that Hambly's open hostility to the Old Cornwall societies would lead to the 'disintegration of the entire Cornish movement'.28

Beer played a major role in resolving this crisis. Anybody who knew Cecil Beer will remember him as a quiet and unassuming gentleman dedicated to the greater cause of his beloved Cornwall. While Hambly comes across as the principal source of friction, it was Beer's diplomatic skills that brought reconciliation. Letters written by

Morton Nance in June 1935 suggest that it was Beer who was responsible for clearing up matters between Tyr ha Tavas and the other societies, and this resulted in Hambly withdrawing the new title of the 'World Cornish Movement'. Nonetheless, Beer shared Hambly's view that the Cornish Movement needed to reach out to the wider community. This was demonstrated by his attitude towards the Gorseth in the 1930s. Whilst some older Revivalists wanted the organisation to remain elitist, Beer felt that the title of bard should not be reserved for services to the language or for really distinguished personalities and should also be awarded for general service to Cornwall, a view, of course, that was eventually accepted.[29] Beer himself was made a bard in 1934 and as more members of Tyr ha Tavas became bards the ideas raised by the youth group became accepted.

However, Beer's active involvement in the Cornish movement was to be disrupted by the outbreak of war. He was posted to a Royal Artillery base in County Durham and, after 'a few frantic weeks of cancelling commitments and advance plans', Tyr ha Tavas became

Map Kenwyn during the Second World War.

13

effectively dormant, although money was deposited in the organisation's post office savings account as late as December 1941.[30] Hambly
was by then an 'up and coming' surgeon in London, while the other
main officers of the group were all relatively young men and liable for
military service. Although the language correspondence circle continued for a while under Cargeeg, the organisation itself went into a state
of abeyance. Surprisingly, Tyr ha Tavas technically remained in existence until as late as July 1980 when it was decided to officially close
the group. Beer consulted some other leading members, including
Talek and Ernest Morton Nance, and it was agreed that their deposit
account, containing a current balance of just over £2.84, should be
closed and the money donated to the Gorseth, as this was the organisation which was closest to the aims of Tyr ha Tavas.[31]

HAIL TO THE HOMELAND: FROM CELTIC REVIVALIST TO TRANS-NATIONAL ICON

The second half of Beer's life also symbolises the wider picture of the
emerging Cornish revival. Whilst the pre-war years saw the development of an essentially cultural movement, which in the case of Tyr ha
Tavas was actually directed by exiles in London, events in the 1950s
and 1960s led to a more political and locally-based revival focused on
the rise of Mebyon Kernow. The popular acceptance of such cultural
icons as St Piran's flag and the Cornish tartan has provided the
imagery for an anti-metropolitan agenda based on practical social and
economic concerns. In recent decades yet another phase in revivalism
can be detected in the export of Celticity from Cornwall to the Cornish
overseas. Payton has remarked on the 'sudden reassertion of an inter-
national Cornish identity' leading to the 'flowering' of Celtic festivals
and Cornish associations in countries from Australia to the United
States of America.[32] On a personal level Beer's service to the Cornish
movement reflects this process. His return to Cornwall in the 1950s
led to a leading role in Mebyon Kernow at a critical time in the evolution of that organisation, while some thirty years later, following his
decision to emigrate to South Australia, Beer assisted in the creation
of the first 'Gathering of the Bards of the Gorseth of Cornwall in
Australia'.

Yet before looking at the wider context we need to consider the personal details of Beer's life. By the end of the war he had been promoted to the rank of Major in the Royal Artillery. Although he expected to return to civilian life, he was instead sent to India where he became Provost Marshall over a large part of that country at a time when it was moving towards independence. Returning to Britain in 1946 he resumed his career with the Civil Service. Before the war this had been with the post office in the London and Home Counties area, but he now embarked on a new challenge. With his wife and two daughters, Margaret and Heather, he now moved to Newport in South Wales where, as District Food Officer in Gwent and then as Meals Organisation Officer for all of Wales, he was effectively in charge of food distribution during the years of rationing and austerity in the late 1940s. Despite his continued absence from the Duchy he continued to take an interest in Cornish affairs, in particular noting the formation of the Young Cornwall group which briefly continued the work of Tyr ha Tavas during the early 1940s. Richard Jenkin, former Grand Bard and president of Mebyon Kernow, who entered Oxford University in 1943, remembers the formation of this organisation:

'I met some people who were actually interested in Cornish and we set up a little organisation (It was intended to be a big organisation but it never grew!) – the Young Cornwall Movement... It intended to take political stances about the problems of Cornwall as well as learning the language and becoming full Cornish Citizens...there was David Balhatchet from Porthcothan near Padstow...there was his girlfriend Mary Foss from Penzance, they eventually married, and there was John Legonna... The Young Cornwall movement was intended to be an organisation of Cornish students and they picked up one or two from other Universities eventually, but communications during war time were difficult and it finally faded out.'[33]

At this stage a combination of increasing ill health and commitments at work meant that there was less time for Beer to return to his active involvement of pre-war days. However, following the onset of heart trouble in the early 1950s he was forced to take early retirement. Just prior to the war he had purchased a plot of ground at Bolingey, which was intended as the site for a retirement home, and he now decided to move to Cornwall. While Beer might have envisaged a peaceful life, this event actually marked the start of a new chapter in his involvement with the Cornish movement when he became chairman of Mebyon Kernow following the resignation of Helena Charles in 1956. The formation of this organisation on 6th January 1951 had marked an official change of direction for the Celtic Revival as the movement now embraced the goal of some form of domestic self-government. Although Beer had been reluctant to embrace a political role in the 1930s, it is significant that he was still influenced by such views. He believed that as the movement grew, with 'more supporting angles', it was inevitable that the idea that Cornwall was historically not part of England and was a nation in itself would lead to a wider acceptance of Cornwall's right to some form of self-government.[34] Mebyon Kernow at that stage was operating as a pressure group, publishing pamphlets and sending letters to the press, and campaigning on a whole series of issues relating to the needs of Cornwall. In that sense it was a natural extension of Beer's pre-war activities.

Map Kenwyn (second from right) at the installation of Talek as Grand Bard at Callington in 1959.

Yet Mebyon Kernow was hardly in the position to lead a campaign for Home Rule. In the first place its activities, like Tyr ha Tavas before the war, were 'hindered by scattered membership'. Quite a number of its leading members, such as Richard Jenkin and Dick Gendall, were either living in England or overseas, which obviously made it difficult to develop a popular image for the movement at the grassroots level.[35] Besides, its curious combination of cultural and political activities, which ensured that the agenda for meetings ranged from such subjects as the need for bilingual paper serviettes to boundary disputes with Devon, prevented Mebyon Kernow from being a more effective nationalist force.[36] Even the way in which Beer took over the chairmanship was testament to the inherent problems within the society. Helena Charles, who had provided the leadership for Mebyon Kernow during the first few years of its existence, had become increasingly frustrated by what she regarded as the 'total apathy' of members. The 'last straw' for Charles came when she lost her St Day seat on Camborne-Redruth UDC. Despite campaigning on a Mebyon Kernow platform, she complained that 'no one with any Cornish nationalist leanings was sufficiently interested to work for me, but the Labour party [represented by 'an unknown upcountryman'] had plenty of canvassers and drivers'.[37] Beer was not even a member of Mebyon Kernow at this time, but when he was approached by some leading activists to become its chairman he decided to accept the invitation in order to assist the group's survival.

Jenkin describes the three years under Beer's leadership as a time of 'quiet but steady growth' for Mebyon Kernow.[38] This is an appropriate remark since this period witnessed the start of a process that was to culminate in the brief popularity of the movement in the late 1960s when it was supported by over 3,000 members. Beer's election as chairman in January 1957 was accompanied by the creation of a 'fresh committee', while Richard and Ann Jenkin took over from Charles as the editors of *New Cornwall*. As an article in that magazine explained in 1958, the return to Cornwall of several activists formerly living in England meant that the group was 'again expanding, with new members and new spheres of activity'. The formation of local branches at this time was another useful development.[39] Moreover, the idea of devolution had been placed on the wider political agenda. This was particularly the case with the local Liberal Party since even in 1952 John Foot, the son of Isaac Foot, supported Mebyon Kernow's demand for Home Rule on the grounds that Cornwall was a 'separate nation'.[40] Similarly, a questionnaire organised by Mebyon Kernow at the time of the 1959 general election found that the Liberal parliamentary candidates in the Duchy were in favour of devolution for Cornwall.[41]

Beer, whilst accepting this more political brand of nationalism, was still determined that nothing should disrupt the unity of the Cornish movement. He was concerned that if Mebyon Kernow adopted a more radical image it might lead to friction with other groups. After all, Morton Nance, Grand Bard of the Cornish Gorseth, was apparently concerned with the political objectives of Mebyon Kernow, and he 'adopted openly a cautiously non-committal attitude' throughout the 1950s.[42] In addition, Beer realised that his chief role in Mebyon Kernow, as with Tyr ha Tavas, was to keep the group together. In Beer's own words, the 'rather determined views' of Charles had caused friction, and he only agreed to preside over the group as caretaker chairman to prevent the organisation from breaking apart.[43] With his wife in poor health he finally handed over the chairmanship of the society to Robert Dunstone in February 1960. For a short period he continued to play an active role in events, such as in October 1960

Cecil Beer, (left) Daphne Nance and Peter Laws at the St Ives Gorseth in 1966.

Cecil Beer being initiated as Deputy Grand Bard at Saltash in 1967.

when he spoke out against a proposal to replace St Piran's cross with a design for a new Cornish flag. Although he withdrew from the executive committee as Mebyon Kernow made the transition in the 1960s from pressure group to political party, he remained a member of the organisation up until his death. Furthermore he still maintained a great interest in Cornish affairs in general and was Gorseth Marshal during the 1950s and 1960s rising to the position of deputy grand bard from 1967 to 1972, to which he was installed at the Saltash Gorseth by Grand Bard George Pawley White. Unfortunately, he had to relinquish this position a year earlier than normal due to ill health to be succeeded in the post by Richard Jenkin. Cecil Beer was also at this time active within the Federation of Old Cornwall Societies.

What can be seen as a major turning point in Map Kenwyn's life occurred in the 1970s when he nearly lost his life following a serious car accident. After being in hospital for several months he was invited to Australia by some friends, and liking life in this new country he decided to settle there permanently. Yet, for Beer, the 12,000 miles that separated him from his native land did not mean that he was to become detached from his beloved Cornwall. Indeed, he can be seen as playing an important part in the process of establishing a Celto-Cornish Identity within the Cornish communities of Australia. During these years the Cornish overseas were gradually turning to a re-invented identity based upon conceptions of the Celticity of their ancestors. As Payton observes about the Cornish trans national communities in North America and Australia, the 're invented identity of contemporary Cornwall became an important resource for those wishing to mobilise Cornish culture as part of the new mode of Cornish multiculturalism. An almost extravagant display of Cornish Tartan and Cornish flags was observable at Cornish events in both continents, with trade stalls invariably doing a brisk trade in artefacts which ranged from Celtic jewellery to Cornish sporrans and tam-o'-shanters.'[44]

Map Kenwyn at Moonta in 1983.

A further opportunity for Australians of Cornish extraction to demonstrate their Cornishness was provided by the Gorseth allowing shortened versions of its ceremony to be performed overseas at Cornish events. During his time in Australia this was a development with which Cecil Beer was to become closely involved, actively encouraging the establishment of an assembly of Australian Cornish bards. In 1985 the then Grand Bard, Hugh Miners (Den Toll), visited Australia as part of a world tour and stayed with Cecil Beer at his home in Gawler. During his visit Den Toll led a Gorseth with eight other robed bards at the Wallaroo Mines at Kadina during the Cornish festival 'Kernewek Lowender'. Included amongst this number was the late Brenda Wootton, the folk singer, who entertained at the four day event. Significantly, for the Cornish revivalist movement this was the first time that a fully robed Grand Bard had conducted the Gorseth ceremony overseas and during this innovative event Den Toll took the opportunity to present to Map Kenwyn an illuminated certificate celebrating his 50 years as a bard of the Cornish Gorseth. The Grand Bard described him in his address as, 'a faithful servant of the Gorsedd and a true son of Cornwall'.

In holding such a ceremony the icons of the new post war Cornish identity were being further cemented into position. Payton observes in his landmark publication, *The Cornish Overseas,* that there was an attempted 'synthesis of Celtic Revivalist and "popular culture", returning afresh to historic sites – engine houses, Methodist Chapels, old cottages, mining landscapes – to co-opt them as icons of new Cornishness. Thus Gorsedd ceremonies have been held amidst the ruined engine houses of Moonta Mines in Australia…'[45] Furthermore, it can also be asserted that by the late 1980s individuals such as Cecil Beer and Ernest Morton Nance had themselves become important living icons of 'Cornishness'. A good example of this occurred in 1988 on the day that the Cornish Gorseth held its diamond jubilee ceremony at Poldhu near Mullion. To mark the event the retiring Grand Bard Richard Jenkin symbolically recreated Marconi's first transatlantic message by telephoning Cecil Beer in Adelaide from the site of the Marconi monument. The *Cornish Guardian* pointed out that 'the message was doubly fitting as five Australians were initiated as Bards during the ceremony which followed in the afternoon.'[46]

This gave added significance to Beer's status at this time as a rare living link with the inter-war revivalist movement.

Shortly before taking the decision to return to Cornwall Map Kenwyn decided to present a plastron or breastplate to be worn by the leader of the ceremony of the bards of the Gorseth of Cornwall in Australia and for this purpose he donated £100 to the Gorseth Kernow. In October 1989 Peter Laws, the Gorseth secretary, wrote to

Richard Jenkin (Grand Bard) talking to Cecil Beer in Australia, by radio on the 70th Anniversary of the first radio transmission from Britain to America.

Beer that 'your letters provoked a long debate at the council on Saturday, and I was asked to express the great gratitude of members for your great generosity. The council agrees as follows:-

1. The Plastron is to be regarded as an addition to the regalia of Gorseth Kernow and is to be on loan to the Bards in Australia.

2. Its custody and insurance will have to be arranged.

3. An Den [Dennis Ivall] is to prepare a design for consideration at the next council meeting on 27th January and it is to incorporate both Celtic Motifs, the Australian acacia... the southern Cross and the word AUSTRALYA. On the reverse side there will be a Cornish Inscription.

After the design is approved, we will have it made in

Cornwall, probably by the Copper Smith who made the new SCOS AN ORSETH. If it is agreeable you will have the ribbon made at your end and or the box.'47

That the plastron was eventually presented to Ron Daw (Map Moonta) at the Marazion Gorseth of 1990 was a gesture that once again originated from the vision of Map Kenwyn. In a short note to Laws he articulated his wish to strengthen the ceremonial aspect of the Australian Cornish revival, writing that 'as the plastron is intended to be and remain the property of the Gorseth Kernow, I think it would be best if it were handed over to Map Moonta at this years Gorseth, **"entrusted to him for safekeeping, on behalf of the Cornish bards in Australia for use at their Bardic assemblies."** (or words to that effect). I cannot be sure of attending the next assembly here which isn't till next year any case. It would put the status of this regalia item on the highest level and apart from any personal angles'.48

Therefore, Map Kenwyn's gift not only symbolised the close kinship ties between a centre of Cornish migration and the 'homeland' but acted as a further representation of the increasing sense of Celticity occurring within the Cornish trans-national communities. The fact that the new plastron was associated with a former Deputy Grand Bard and pioneer member of Tyr ha Tavas further served to give a Celtic authenticity to what after all is a comparatively modern Cornish tradition being practiced in a young nation still desperately trying to come to grips with its own identity. The continuing quest for a Cornish identity which Beer himself had embarked on some sixty years previously was now being taken up enthusiastically in communities thousands of miles from Cornish shores. This was described in a letter from Map Moonta to Map Kenwyn recounting the events of the 1991 Kernewek Lowender.

'...to my way of thinking it was perhaps the most successful yet, with wonderful attendances at all events. The former Friday 'Cornish language afternoon' was extended to encompass family History, books on Cornwall and a table with books on the language with special reference to derivation of family and place names. The meet the

Cornish evening was transferred to the Wallaroo Town Hall, and attracted about 350-400 people. Messages of greeting were read from various folk in the U.K...The Bardic ceremony was performed by solely Australian bards and (quite appropriately I thought) I had the honour of wearing the new plastron as leader of the ceremony...the number of spectators doubled to 350-400 from 1989, and so the gathering is now firmly established as one of the outstanding highlights of the Lowender, besides significantly increasing its "Cornishness".[49]

Ron Daw (Map Moonta) wearing the Plastron donated by Map Kenwyn, 1991.

However, in 1990 Map Kenwyn had to leave Australia to live in Newquay with his eldest daughter, Margaret Trewartha. Now in his late eighties and in poor health he was increasingly unable to participate in Cornish affairs, and had to abandon his plans to write a book on the history of Tyr ha Tavas, which would obviously have been invaluable to researchers. Nevertheless, despite the frailty of his body, his mind remained active and he was very willing to share his memories of the period. He continued as a member of a number of Cornish organisations, and was an avid reader of Mebyon Kernow's magazine, *Cornish Nation*. The Cornish Gorseth was to honour him one further time. At the rain-affected 1994 Gorseth held at Camborne Cecil Beer and Ernest Morton Nance were presented with illuminated certificates, prepared by Dennis Ivall (An Den), to celebrate sixty years bardship and service. This event, four years before his death, was a fitting mark of respect for Beer's work on behalf of Cornwall and the Cornish Diaspora.

CONCLUSION

During his long lifetime Map Kenwyn witnessed the spectacular growth of the Cornish movement. He had been initiated into the Gorseth Kernow at Mordon's first ceremony as Grand Bard and had lived to see the appointment of Ann Trevenen Jenkin as the first female Grand Bard of any of the Celtic Gorsethow. He was very much a symbol of the changing nature of the Celto-Cornish Revival, moving away from antiquarian concerns to the wider interests of the Cornish people and this was demonstrated in his attitude towards organisations from the Gorseth to the Federation of Old Cornwall societies. His service to the movement in Australia during the 1980s is a reminder of the 'Greater Cornwall' outside the Homeland. One could add that the personal significance of his 'backroom boy' approach within the ranks of the often fractious proto-nationalist organisations, both before and after the Second World War, was that he helped to ensure the survival of the Revival itself. His quiet but efficient demeanour provided the essential stability that nurtured both Tyr ha Tavas and Mebyon Kernow during their formative years. Indeed, perhaps the best way to remember Cecil Beer is actually his own tribute to Robert Morton Nance in 1959 since the same words obviously apply to Beer as well:

> 'I will always consider it his lasting wish that branches of the Cornish Movement should keep in harmony with one another, in tolerance of each others opinions, having but one ultimate aim, – unity and the preservation of our Cornish Nationhood. What more fitting message could he have left the Cornish people?'[50]

NOTES AND REFERENCES

1 Information from Margaret Trewartha (nee. Beer); Our thanks to Margaret for her general assistance with photographs and papers relating to her father. Bardic biographical information, Gorseth Kernow Archive.

2 Cecil Beer papers, notes written by Beer for a planned book on the history of Tyr ha Tavas.

3 Cecil Beer papers, *ibid.*

4 Recorded interview between Garry Tregidga and Cecil Beer, CAVA 25 November 1996.

5 P. Payton, *The Making of Modern Cornwall: Historical Experience and the Persistence of "Difference"*, Redruth, 1992, p.132.

6 CAVA interview with Beer, 25 November 1996; *Cornish Guardian*, 17 August 1933

7 *The Western Morning News*, September 1st 1933

8 *Ibid.*

9 Tyr Ha Tavas papers at the Institute of Cornish Studies.

10 *The Cornish Times*, September 5th 1935.

11 *The Cornish Guardian*, September 5th 1935.

12 Beer papers, Tredynek (Francis Tredinnick) to Map Kenwyn (Beer), 3 June 1935.

13 John Jenkin interview with Treve Crago CAVA 8-2-2000.

14 CAVA interview with Beer, 25th November 1996.

15 *The Cornish Times*, September 14th. 1934

16 *Ibid.*

17 For further information see Garry Tregidga, 'The Politics of the Celto-Cornish Revival, 1886-1939'. in P Payton (ed.) *Cornish Studies: Five*, Exeter, 1997.

18 Beer papers, letter from Mordon to Map Kenwyn, 24th June 1935.

19 Diary of Edwin Chirgwin (February 1933) in the possession of John Jenkin.

20 Undated Tyr ha Tavas Papers at the Institute of Cornish Studies.

21 CAVA interview with Beer 25th November 1996; *Cornish Guardian* 30th May 1935.

22 Beer Papers, *Cornish Guardian*, 25th August 1938; see also E.G Retallack Hooper to Beer 3rd July 1935.

23 CAVA interview with Beer, 25th November 1996.

24 CAVA interview with Richard Jenkin, 14th February 2000.

25 Rowse Papers (University of Exeter Library) *Cornish Labour News*, Dec 1932, No.3.

26 *Cornish Labour News*, May 1937. No.56; Rowse papers, newspaper cuttings from the *West Briton* 20th August 1936 and 7th October 1937.

27 CAVA interview with Beer, 25th November 1996.

28 Beer Papers, Nance to Beer, 10th June 1935.

29 Interview with Beer, 25th November 1996.

30 Beer Papers, notes written by Beer for a planned book on *Tyr ha Tavas*.

31 Letter from Cecil Beer to the Director of the National Savings Bank 9th July 1980.

32 Philip Payton, *The Cornish Overseas,* Fowey, 1999, p.392.

33 CAVA interview with Richard Jenkin, 14th February 2000

34 CAVA interview with Beer, 25th November 1996.

35 *New Cornwall,* Vol.6, No.6 (October-November 1958), p.7.

36 Leonard Truran papers (Institute of Cornish Studies), minutes of Mebyon Kernow meeting, 8th October 1960.

37 Truran papers, undated memorandum from Helena Charles to Mebyon Kernow members, c. 1956.

38 R. Jenkin, *40 Years of Mebyon Kernow* (MK, 1991), p.4.

39 *New Cornwall,* Vol., No.2 (February-March 1957), p.4; *New Cornwall,* Vol. 6, No.6 (October-November 1958), p.7.

40 *Cornish Guardian,* 6 May 1952.

41 *New Cornwall,* Vol.7, No. 6 (October-November 1959), pp.8-9

42 *New Cornwall,* Vol.7, No.5 (August-September 1959), p. 4.

43 CAVA interview with Beer, 25 November 1996

44 Philip Payton, *The Cornish Overseas,* Fowey 1999, p.395.

45 *Ibid,* p.396

46 *The Cornish Guardian,* September 8th 1988.

47 Letter from Peter Laws to Cecil Beer, October 1989 (Gorseth Kernow Archive).

48 Note from Beer to Laws, October 1989, the Beer Papers

49 Letter from Ron Daw to Cecil Beer 12-6-1991 (Gorseth Kernow Archive).

50 *New Cornwall,* Vol.7, No.5, (August-September 1959), p.4.

About the Authors

Dr Garry Tregidga is Deputy Director of the Institute of Cornish Studies and Project Director of the Cornish Audio Visual Archive (CAVA), as well as Chairman of the Cornish History Network. Current research interests include the development of Cornish party politics since the 1880s in a Celtic and European context, Methodism and society in Cornwall, oral history and ethnomusicology. His recent work includes a major political study, entitled *The Liberal Party in South West Britain since 1918: Political Decline,Dormancy and Rebirth*, which has just been published by the University of Exeter.

Treve Crago is researcher/historian for the Gorsedd Kernow Archival Survey Project and is also a postgraduate student at the Institute of Cornish Studies, where he is Senior Researcher for the Cornish Audio Visual Archive, as well as Network representative for Cornwall for the Oral History Society. His more recent writings include 'Highlighting the Social Dynamics of Oral History: An investigation into the changing senses of identity within Cornish communities between the World Wars' which is to be shortly published by the Confederation Internationale de Genealogie et d'Heraldique (CIGH).